THIS JOURNAL BELONGS TO

Prompts to start brainstorming

1. Thankful for my family
2. Thankful for my friends
3. Thankful for my home
4. Thankful for my teacher
5. Thankful for my pet
6. Thankful for being able to help someone
7. Thankful for kind words said to me
8. Thankful for making someone happy
9. Thankful for something new I learned today
10. Thankful that I can smell nice things
11. Thankful for what makes me different
12. Thankful for things that make me laugh

TODAY IS _____

I'M THANKFUL FOR...

1. _____
2. _____
3. _____

SOMETHING I LEARNED TODAY

_____

(DRAW OR WRITE) HOW DO I FEEL TODAY?

(DRAW OR WRITE)
WHAT WAS THE BEST PART OF MY DAY?

TODAY IS _____ / / _____

I'M THANKFUL FOR...

1. _____

2. _____

3. _____

SOMETHING I LEARNED TODAY

_____

(DRAW OR WRITE) HOW DO I FEEL TODAY?

(DRAW OR WRITE)
WHAT WAS THE BEST PART OF MY DAY?

TODAY IS _____ / / _____

I'M THANKFUL FOR...

1. _____

2. _____

3. _____

SOMETHING I LEARNED TODAY

_____

(DRAW OR WRITE) HOW DO I FEEL TODAY?

(DRAW OR WRITE)
WHAT WAS THE BEST PART OF MY DAY?

TODAY IS _____ / / _____

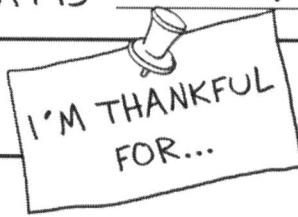

I'M THANKFUL FOR...

1. _____

2. _____

3. _____

SOMETHING I LEARNED TODAY

_____

(DRAW OR WRITE) HOW DO I FEEL TODAY?

(DRAW OR WRITE)
WHAT WAS THE BEST PART OF MY DAY?

TODAY IS _____ / _____ / _____

I'M THANKFUL FOR...

1.

2.

3.

SOMETHING I LEARNED TODAY

(DRAW OR WRITE)
HOW DO I FEEL TODAY?

WHAT WAS
THE BEST
PART OF MY
DAY?

THIS
PERSON
BROUGHT ME
JOY TODAY

TODAY IS _____

I'M THANKFUL FOR...

1. _____

2. _____

3. _____

SOMETHING I LEARNED TODAY

_____

(DRAW OR WRITE) HOW DO I FEEL TODAY?

(DRAW OR WRITE)
WHAT WAS THE BEST PART OF MY DAY?

TODAY IS _____ / / _____

I'M THANKFUL FOR...

1. _____
2. _____
3. _____

SOMETHING I LEARNED TODAY
_____

(DRAW OR WRITE) HOW DO I FEEL TODAY?

(DRAW OR WRITE)
WHAT WAS THE BEST PART OF MY DAY?

TODAY IS _____ / /_____

I'M THANKFUL FOR...

1. _____
2. _____
3. _____

SOMETHING I LEARNED TODAY
_____

(DRAW OR WRITE) HOW DO I FEEL TODAY?

(DRAW OR WRITE)
WHAT WAS THE BEST PART OF MY DAY?

TODAY IS _____ / ___ / ___

I'M THANKFUL FOR...

1. _____
2. _____
3. _____

💡 SOMETHING I LEARNED TODAY
_____

(DRAW OR WRITE) HOW DO I FEEL TODAY?

(DRAW OR WRITE)
WHAT WAS THE BEST PART OF MY DAY?

LET'S DO THIS

TODAY IS _____

I'M THANKFUL FOR...

1. _____
2. _____
3. _____

SOMETHING I LEARNED TODAY
_____

(DRAW OR WRITE) HOW DO I FEEL TODAY?

(DRAW OR WRITE)
WHAT WAS THE BEST PART OF MY DAY?

TODAY IS _____ / /

I'M THANKFUL FOR...

1. _____
2. _____
3. _____

SOMETHING I LEARNED TODAY

_____

(DRAW OR WRITE) HOW DO I FEEL TODAY?

(DRAW OR WRITE)
WHAT WAS THE BEST PART OF MY DAY?

TODAY IS ___ / ___ / ___

I'M THANKFUL FOR...

1.

2.

3.

SOMETHING I LEARNED TODAY

(DRAW OR WRITE)
HOW DO I FEEL TODAY?

WHAT WAS THE BEST PART OF MY DAY?

THIS PERSON BROUGHT ME JOY TODAY

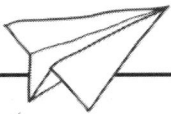

TODAY IS _____

I'M THANKFUL FOR...

1. _____
2. _____
3. _____

SOMETHING I LEARNED TODAY

_____

(DRAW OR WRITE) HOW DO I FEEL TODAY?

(DRAW OR WRITE)
WHAT WAS THE BEST PART OF MY DAY?

TODAY IS _____ / /_____

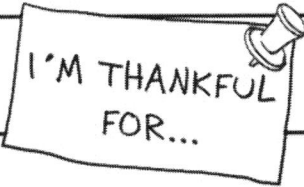
I'M THANKFUL FOR...

1. _____
2. _____
3. _____

SOMETHING I LEARNED TODAY
_____

(DRAW OR WRITE) HOW DO I FEEL TODAY?

(DRAW OR WRITE)
WHAT WAS THE BEST PART OF MY DAY?

TODAY IS _____ / /

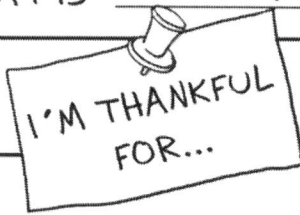
I'M THANKFUL FOR...

1. _____
2. _____
3. _____

SOMETHING I LEARNED TODAY

_____

(DRAW OR WRITE) HOW DO I FEEL TODAY?

(DRAW OR WRITE)
WHAT WAS THE BEST PART OF MY DAY?

TODAY IS _____ / / _____

I'M THANKFUL FOR...

1. _____

2. _____

3. _____

SOMETHING I LEARNED TODAY

_____

(DRAW OR WRITE) HOW DO I FEEL TODAY?

(DRAW OR WRITE)
WHAT WAS THE BEST PART OF MY DAY?

TODAY IS ___ / ___ / ___

I'M THANKFUL FOR...

1.

2.

3.

SOMETHING I LEARNED TODAY

**(DRAW OR WRITE)
HOW DO I FEEL TODAY?**

WHAT WAS THE BEST PART OF MY DAY?

THIS PERSON BROUGHT ME JOY TODAY

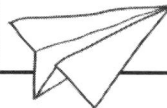

TODAY IS _____

I'M THANKFUL
FOR...

1. _____
2. _____
3. _____

SOMETHING I LEARNED TODAY
_____

(DRAW OR WRITE) HOW DO I FEEL TODAY?

(DRAW OR WRITE)
WHAT WAS THE BEST PART OF MY DAY?

great tHiNGS
NEVER
Came from
COMFORT
ZONES

TODAY IS _____ / / _____

I'M THANKFUL FOR...

1. _____

2. _____

3. _____

SOMETHING I LEARNED TODAY

_____

(DRAW OR WRITE) HOW DO I FEEL TODAY?

(DRAW OR WRITE)
WHAT WAS THE BEST PART OF MY DAY?

TODAY IS _____ / / _____

I'M THANKFUL FOR...

1. _____

2. _____

3. _____

SOMETHING I LEARNED TODAY

_____

(DRAW OR WRITE) HOW DO I FEEL TODAY?

(DRAW OR WRITE)
WHAT WAS THE BEST PART OF MY DAY?

TODAY IS _____ / / _____

I'M THANKFUL FOR...

1. _____
2. _____
3. _____

SOMETHING I LEARNED TODAY
_____

(DRAW OR WRITE) HOW DO I FEEL TODAY?

(DRAW OR WRITE)
WHAT WAS THE BEST PART OF MY DAY?

TODAY IS ___ / /___

I'M THANKFUL FOR...

1.

2.

3.

SOMETHING I LEARNED TODAY

(DRAW OR WRITE)
HOW DO I FEEL TODAY?

WHAT WAS
THE BEST
PART OF MY
DAY?

THIS
PERSON
BROUGHT ME
JOY TODAY

TODAY IS _____

I'M THANKFUL FOR...

1. _____
2. _____
3. _____

SOMETHING I LEARNED TODAY

_____

(DRAW OR WRITE) HOW DO I FEEL TODAY?

(DRAW OR WRITE)
WHAT WAS THE BEST PART OF MY DAY?

TODAY IS _____ / /

I'M THANKFUL FOR...

1. _____
2. _____
3. _____

SOMETHING I LEARNED TODAY

_____

(DRAW OR WRITE) HOW DO I FEEL TODAY?

(DRAW OR WRITE)
WHAT WAS THE BEST PART OF MY DAY?

TODAY IS _____ / / _____

I'M THANKFUL FOR...

1. _____

2. _____

3. _____

SOMETHING I LEARNED TODAY

_____

(DRAW OR WRITE) HOW DO I FEEL TODAY?

(DRAW OR WRITE)
WHAT WAS THE BEST PART OF MY DAY?

TODAY IS _____ / ___ / ___

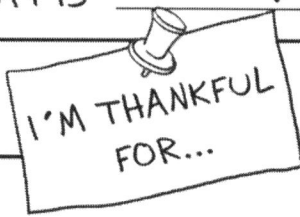

I'M THANKFUL FOR...

1. _____
2. _____
3. _____

SOMETHING I LEARNED TODAY

_____

(DRAW OR WRITE) HOW DO I FEEL TODAY?

(DRAW OR WRITE)
WHAT WAS THE BEST PART OF MY DAY?

TODAY IS _____ / _____ / _____

I'M THANKFUL FOR...

1.

2.

3.

SOMETHING I LEARNED TODAY

(DRAW OR WRITE)
HOW DO I FEEL TODAY?

WHAT WAS THE BEST PART OF MY DAY?

THIS PERSON BROUGHT ME JOY TODAY

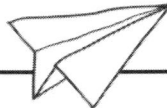

believe
in yourself

TODAY IS _____

I'M THANKFUL FOR...

1. _____
2. _____
3. _____

SOMETHING I LEARNED TODAY
_____

(DRAW OR WRITE) HOW DO I FEEL TODAY?

(DRAW OR WRITE)
WHAT WAS THE BEST PART OF MY DAY?

TODAY IS _____ / / _____

I'M THANKFUL FOR...

1. _____
2. _____
3. _____

SOMETHING I LEARNED TODAY

_____

(DRAW OR WRITE) HOW DO I FEEL TODAY?

(DRAW OR WRITE)
WHAT WAS THE BEST PART OF MY DAY?

TODAY IS ___ / ___ / ___

I'M THANKFUL FOR...

1. _____
2. _____
3. _____

SOMETHING I LEARNED TODAY

_____

(DRAW OR WRITE) HOW DO I FEEL TODAY?

(DRAW OR WRITE)
WHAT WAS THE BEST PART OF MY DAY?

TODAY IS ___ / ___ / ___

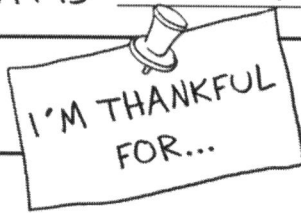

I'M THANKFUL FOR...

1. _____
2. _____
3. _____

💡 SOMETHING I LEARNED TODAY

_____

(DRAW OR WRITE) HOW DO I FEEL TODAY?

(DRAW OR WRITE)
WHAT WAS THE BEST PART OF MY DAY?

TODAY IS ___/___/___

I'M THANKFUL FOR...

1.

2.

3.

SOMETHING I LEARNED TODAY

(DRAW OR WRITE)
HOW DO I FEEL TODAY?

WHAT WAS
THE BEST
PART OF MY
DAY?

THIS
PERSON
BROUGHT ME
JOY TODAY

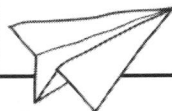

TODAY IS _____

I'M THANKFUL FOR...

1. _____

2. _____

3. _____

SOMETHING I LEARNED TODAY

_____

(DRAW OR WRITE) HOW DO I FEEL TODAY?

(DRAW OR WRITE)
WHAT WAS THE BEST PART OF MY DAY?

TODAY IS _____ / / _____

I'M THANKFUL FOR...

1. _____
2. _____
3. _____

SOMETHING I LEARNED TODAY

_____

(DRAW OR WRITE) HOW DO I FEEL TODAY?

(DRAW OR WRITE)
WHAT WAS THE BEST PART OF MY DAY?

TODAY IS _____

I'M THANKFUL FOR...

1. _____
2. _____
3. _____

SOMETHING I LEARNED TODAY
_____

(DRAW OR WRITE) HOW DO I FEEL TODAY?

(DRAW OR WRITE)
WHAT WAS THE BEST PART OF MY DAY?

TODAY IS _____ / /

I'M THANKFUL FOR...

1. _____

2. _____

3. _____

SOMETHING I LEARNED TODAY

_____

(DRAW OR WRITE) HOW DO I FEEL TODAY?

(DRAW OR WRITE)
WHAT WAS THE BEST PART OF MY DAY?

TODAY IS _____ / ___ / ___

I'M THANKFUL FOR...

1. _____
2. _____
3. _____

SOMETHING I LEARNED TODAY

_____

(DRAW OR WRITE) HOW DO I FEEL TODAY?

(DRAW OR WRITE)
WHAT WAS THE BEST PART OF MY DAY?

TODAY IS _____ / /

I'M THANKFUL FOR...

1. _____

2. _____

3. _____

💡 SOMETHING I LEARNED TODAY

_____

(DRAW OR WRITE) HOW DO I FEEL TODAY?

(DRAW OR WRITE)
WHAT WAS THE BEST PART OF MY DAY?

TODAY IS ___ / ___ / ___

I'M THANKFUL FOR...

1.

2.

3.

SOMETHING I LEARNED TODAY

(DRAW OR WRITE)
HOW DO I FEEL TODAY?

WHAT WAS THE BEST PART OF MY DAY?

THIS PERSON BROUGHT ME JOY TODAY

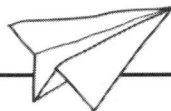

TODAY IS _____

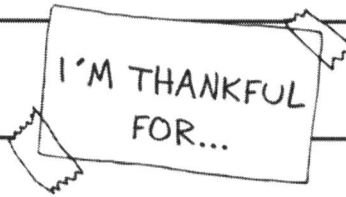

I'M THANKFUL FOR...

1. _____

2. _____

3. _____

SOMETHING I LEARNED TODAY

_____

(DRAW OR WRITE) HOW DO I FEEL TODAY?

(DRAW OR WRITE)
WHAT WAS THE BEST PART OF MY DAY?

TODAY IS _____ / ____ / _____

I'M THANKFUL FOR...

1. _____

2. _____

3. _____

SOMETHING I LEARNED TODAY

_____

(DRAW OR WRITE) HOW DO I FEEL TODAY?

(DRAW OR WRITE)
WHAT WAS THE BEST PART OF MY DAY?

TODAY IS _____ / / _____

I'M THANKFUL FOR...

1. _____
2. _____
3. _____

SOMETHING I LEARNED TODAY

_____

(DRAW OR WRITE) HOW DO I FEEL TODAY?

(DRAW OR WRITE)
WHAT WAS THE BEST PART OF MY DAY?

TODAY IS ___ / ___ / ___

I'M THANKFUL FOR...

1. _____

2. _____

3. _____

SOMETHING I LEARNED TODAY

_____

(DRAW OR WRITE) HOW DO I FEEL TODAY?

(DRAW OR WRITE)
WHAT WAS THE BEST PART OF MY DAY?

great THINGS
NEVER
came from
COMFORT
ZONES

TODAY IS ___ / / ___

I'M THANKFUL FOR...

1.

2.

3.

SOMETHING I LEARNED TODAY

(DRAW OR WRITE)
HOW DO I FEEL TODAY?

WHAT WAS
THE BEST
PART OF MY
DAY?

THIS
PERSON
BROUGHT ME
JOY TODAY

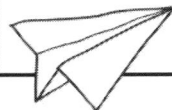

TODAY IS _____

I'M THANKFUL FOR...

1. _____

2. _____

3. _____

SOMETHING I LEARNED TODAY

_____

(DRAW OR WRITE) HOW DO I FEEL TODAY?

(DRAW OR WRITE)
WHAT WAS THE BEST PART OF MY DAY?

TODAY IS _____ / / _____

I'M THANKFUL FOR...

1. _____

2. _____

3. _____

SOMETHING I LEARNED TODAY

_____

(DRAW OR WRITE) HOW DO I FEEL TODAY?

(DRAW OR WRITE)
WHAT WAS THE BEST PART OF MY DAY?

TODAY IS ___/___/___

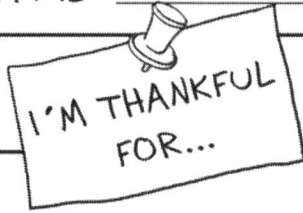
I'M THANKFUL FOR...

1. _____

2. _____

3. _____

💡 SOMETHING I LEARNED TODAY

_____

(DRAW OR WRITE) HOW DO I FEEL TODAY?

(DRAW OR WRITE)
WHAT WAS THE BEST PART OF MY DAY?

TODAY IS ___ / / _____

I'M THANKFUL FOR...

1. _____
2. _____
3. _____

💡 SOMETHING I LEARNED TODAY

_____

(DRAW OR WRITE) HOW DO I FEEL TODAY?

(DRAW OR WRITE)
WHAT WAS THE BEST PART OF MY DAY?

TODAY IS ___ / ___ / ___

I'M THANKFUL FOR...

1.

2.

3.

SOMETHING I LEARNED TODAY

(DRAW OR WRITE)
HOW DO I FEEL TODAY?

WHAT WAS
THE BEST
PART OF MY
DAY?

THIS
PERSON
BROUGHT ME
JOY TODAY

TODAY IS _____

I'M THANKFUL FOR...

1. _____
2. _____
3. _____

SOMETHING I LEARNED TODAY

_____

(DRAW OR WRITE) HOW DO I FEEL TODAY?

(DRAW OR WRITE)
WHAT WAS THE BEST PART OF MY DAY?

TODAY IS _____ / __ / __

I'M THANKFUL FOR...

1. _____

2. _____

3. _____

SOMETHING I LEARNED TODAY

_____

(DRAW OR WRITE) HOW DO I FEEL TODAY?

(DRAW OR WRITE)
WHAT WAS THE BEST PART OF MY DAY?

TODAY IS ___ / ___ / ___

I'M THANKFUL FOR...

1. _____
2. _____
3. _____

SOMETHING I LEARNED TODAY

_____

(DRAW OR WRITE) HOW DO I FEEL TODAY?

(DRAW OR WRITE)
WHAT WAS THE BEST PART OF MY DAY?

TODAY IS ____ / ____ / ____

I'M THANKFUL FOR...

1. _____

2. _____

3. _____

SOMETHING I LEARNED TODAY

_____

(DRAW OR WRITE) HOW DO I FEEL TODAY?

(DRAW OR WRITE)
WHAT WAS THE BEST PART OF MY DAY?

TODAY IS _____ / _____ / _____

I'M THANKFUL FOR...

1.

2.

3.

SOMETHING I LEARNED TODAY

(DRAW OR WRITE)
HOW DO I FEEL TODAY?

WHAT WAS
THE BEST
PART OF MY
DAY?

THIS
PERSON
BROUGHT ME
JOY TODAY

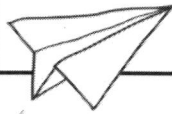

TODAY IS _____

I'M THANKFUL
FOR...

1. _____
2. _____
3. _____

SOMETHING I LEARNED TODAY

_____

(DRAW OR WRITE) HOW DO I FEEL TODAY?

(DRAW OR WRITE)
WHAT WAS THE BEST PART OF MY DAY?

TODAY IS _____ / /_____

I'M THANKFUL FOR...

1. _____

2. _____

3. _____

SOMETHING I LEARNED TODAY

_____

(DRAW OR WRITE) HOW DO I FEEL TODAY?

(DRAW OR WRITE)
WHAT WAS THE BEST PART OF MY DAY?

TODAY IS _____ / / _____

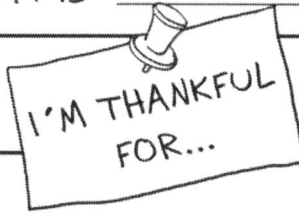

I'M THANKFUL FOR...

1. _____
2. _____
3. _____

💡 SOMETHING I LEARNED TODAY

_____

(DRAW OR WRITE) HOW DO I FEEL TODAY?

(DRAW OR WRITE)
WHAT WAS THE BEST PART OF MY DAY?

TODAY IS _____ / _____ / _____

I'M THANKFUL FOR...

1. _____

2. _____

3. _____

SOMETHING I LEARNED TODAY

_____

(DRAW OR WRITE) HOW DO I FEEL TODAY?

(DRAW OR WRITE)
WHAT WAS THE BEST PART OF MY DAY?

TODAY IS _____ / _____ / _____

I'M THANKFUL FOR...

1.

2.

3.

SOMETHING I LEARNED TODAY

(DRAW OR WRITE)
HOW DO I FEEL TODAY?

WHAT WAS THE BEST PART OF MY DAY?

THIS PERSON BROUGHT ME JOY TODAY

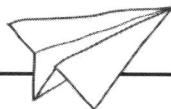

TODAY IS _____

I'M THANKFUL FOR...

1. _____
2. _____
3. _____

SOMETHING I LEARNED TODAY

_____

(DRAW OR WRITE) HOW DO I FEEL TODAY?

(DRAW OR WRITE)
WHAT WAS THE BEST PART OF MY DAY?

TODAY IS _____ / /

I'M THANKFUL FOR...

1. _____
2. _____
3. _____

SOMETHING I LEARNED TODAY

_____

(DRAW OR WRITE) HOW DO I FEEL TODAY?

(DRAW OR WRITE)
WHAT WAS THE BEST PART OF MY DAY?

TODAY IS ___ / ___ / ___

I'M THANKFUL FOR...

1. _____
2. _____
3. _____

SOMETHING I LEARNED TODAY

_____

(DRAW OR WRITE) HOW DO I FEEL TODAY?

(DRAW OR WRITE)
WHAT WAS THE BEST PART OF MY DAY?

LET'S DO THIS

TODAY IS ___ / ___ / ___

I'M THANKFUL FOR...

1. _____
2. _____
3. _____

SOMETHING I LEARNED TODAY

_____

(DRAW OR WRITE) HOW DO I FEEL TODAY?

(DRAW OR WRITE)
WHAT WAS THE BEST PART OF MY DAY?

TODAY IS _____

I'M THANKFUL FOR...

1. _____
2. _____
3. _____

SOMETHING I LEARNED TODAY

_____

(DRAW OR WRITE) HOW DO I FEEL TODAY?

(DRAW OR WRITE)
WHAT WAS THE BEST PART OF MY DAY?

TODAY IS _____ / / _____

I'M THANKFUL FOR...

1. _____

2. _____

3. _____

SOMETHING I LEARNED TODAY

_____

(DRAW OR WRITE) HOW DO I FEEL TODAY?

(DRAW OR WRITE)
WHAT WAS THE BEST PART OF MY DAY?

TODAY IS _____ / /

I'M THANKFUL FOR...

1. _____

2. _____

3. _____

SOMETHING I LEARNED TODAY

_____

(DRAW OR WRITE) HOW DO I FEEL TODAY?

(DRAW OR WRITE)
WHAT WAS THE BEST PART OF MY DAY?

TODAY IS _____ / ___ / _____

I'M THANKFUL FOR...

1. _____
2. _____
3. _____

SOMETHING I LEARNED TODAY
_____

(DRAW OR WRITE) HOW DO I FEEL TODAY?

(DRAW OR WRITE)
WHAT WAS THE BEST PART OF MY DAY?

TODAY IS ___ / /

I'M THANKFUL FOR...

1.

2.

3.

SOMETHING I LEARNED TODAY

(DRAW OR WRITE)
HOW DO I FEEL TODAY?

WHAT WAS
THE BEST
PART OF MY
DAY?

THIS
PERSON
BROUGHT ME
JOY TODAY

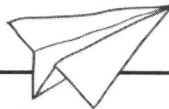

TODAY IS _____

I'M THANKFUL
FOR...

1. _____
2. _____
3. _____

SOMETHING I LEARNED TODAY
_____

(DRAW OR WRITE) HOW DO I FEEL TODAY?

(DRAW OR WRITE)
WHAT WAS THE BEST PART OF MY DAY?

TODAY IS _____ / /

I'M THANKFUL FOR...

1. _____
2. _____
3. _____

SOMETHING I LEARNED TODAY

_____

(DRAW OR WRITE) HOW DO I FEEL TODAY?

(DRAW OR WRITE)
WHAT WAS THE BEST PART OF MY DAY?

TODAY IS _____ / _____ / _____

I'M THANKFUL FOR...

1. _____

2. _____

3. _____

💡 SOMETHING I LEARNED TODAY

_____

(DRAW OR WRITE) HOW DO I FEEL TODAY?

👍 (DRAW OR WRITE)
WHAT WAS THE BEST PART OF MY DAY?

TODAY IS _____ / /

I'M THANKFUL FOR...

1. _____
2. _____
3. _____

SOMETHING I LEARNED TODAY

_____

(DRAW OR WRITE) HOW DO I FEEL TODAY?

(DRAW OR WRITE)
WHAT WAS THE BEST PART OF MY DAY?

TODAY IS ___/___/___

I'M THANKFUL FOR...

1.

2.

3.

SOMETHING I LEARNED TODAY

(DRAW OR WRITE)
HOW DO I FEEL TODAY?

WHAT WAS
THE BEST
PART OF MY
DAY?

THIS
PERSON
BROUGHT ME
JOY TODAY

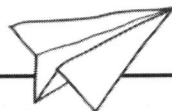

TODAY IS _____

I'M THANKFUL FOR...

1. _____
2. _____
3. _____

SOMETHING I LEARNED TODAY
_____

(DRAW OR WRITE) HOW DO I FEEL TODAY?

(DRAW OR WRITE)
WHAT WAS THE BEST PART OF MY DAY?

TODAY IS _____ / / _____

I'M THANKFUL FOR...

1. _____
2. _____
3. _____

SOMETHING I LEARNED TODAY

_____

(DRAW OR WRITE) HOW DO I FEEL TODAY?

(DRAW OR WRITE)
WHAT WAS THE BEST PART OF MY DAY?

TODAY IS _____ / /

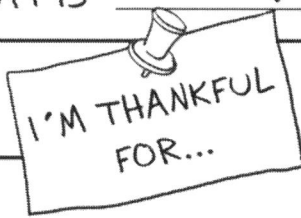
I'M THANKFUL FOR...

1. _____
2. _____
3. _____

SOMETHING I LEARNED TODAY
_____

(DRAW OR WRITE) HOW DO I FEEL TODAY?

(DRAW OR WRITE)
WHAT WAS THE BEST PART OF MY DAY?

TODAY IS ___ / /_____

I'M THANKFUL FOR...

1. _____
2. _____
3. _____

SOMETHING I LEARNED TODAY
_____

(DRAW OR WRITE) HOW DO I FEEL TODAY?

(DRAW OR WRITE)
WHAT WAS THE BEST PART OF MY DAY?

believe

in yourself

TODAY IS ___ / ___ / ___

I'M THANKFUL FOR...

1.

2.

3.

SOMETHING I LEARNED TODAY

(DRAW OR WRITE)
HOW DO I FEEL TODAY?

WHAT WAS THE BEST PART OF MY DAY?

THIS PERSON BROUGHT ME JOY TODAY

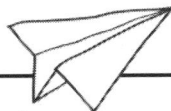

TODAY IS _____

I'M THANKFUL FOR...

1. _____
2. _____
3. _____

SOMETHING I LEARNED TODAY

_____

(DRAW OR WRITE) HOW DO I FEEL TODAY?

(DRAW OR WRITE)
WHAT WAS THE BEST PART OF MY DAY?

TODAY IS _____ / / _____

I'M THANKFUL FOR...

1. _____

2. _____

3. _____

SOMETHING I LEARNED TODAY

_____

(DRAW OR WRITE) HOW DO I FEEL TODAY?

(DRAW OR WRITE)
WHAT WAS THE BEST PART OF MY DAY?

TODAY IS _____ / / _____

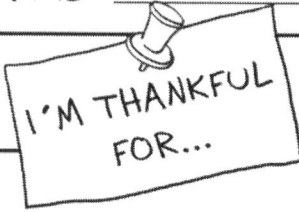
I'M THANKFUL FOR...

1. _____
2. _____
3. _____

💡 SOMETHING I LEARNED TODAY
_____

(DRAW OR WRITE) HOW DO I FEEL TODAY?

(DRAW OR WRITE)
WHAT WAS THE BEST PART OF MY DAY?

TODAY IS ___ / ___ / ___

I'M THANKFUL FOR...

1. _____

2. _____

3. _____

SOMETHING I LEARNED TODAY

_____

(DRAW OR WRITE) HOW DO I FEEL TODAY?

(DRAW OR WRITE)
WHAT WAS THE BEST PART OF MY DAY?

TODAY IS _____ / /

I'M THANKFUL FOR...

1.

2.

3.

SOMETHING I LEARNED TODAY

(DRAW OR WRITE)
HOW DO I FEEL TODAY?

WHAT WAS
THE BEST
PART OF MY
DAY?

THIS
PERSON
BROUGHT ME
JOY TODAY

TODAY IS _____

I'M THANKFUL FOR...

1. _____
2. _____
3. _____

SOMETHING I LEARNED TODAY

_____

(DRAW OR WRITE) HOW DO I FEEL TODAY?

(DRAW OR WRITE)
WHAT WAS THE BEST PART OF MY DAY?

TODAY IS _____ / / _____

I'M THANKFUL FOR...

1. _____

2. _____

3. _____

SOMETHING I LEARNED TODAY

_____

(DRAW OR WRITE) HOW DO I FEEL TODAY?

(DRAW OR WRITE)
WHAT WAS THE BEST PART OF MY DAY?

TODAY IS _____ / ___ / ___

I'M THANKFUL FOR...

1. _____
2. _____
3. _____

SOMETHING I LEARNED TODAY

_____

(DRAW OR WRITE) HOW DO I FEEL TODAY?

(DRAW OR WRITE)
WHAT WAS THE BEST PART OF MY DAY?

TODAY IS _____ / /

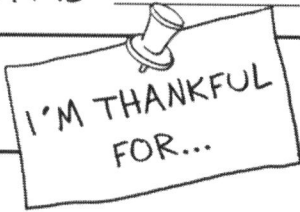

I'M THANKFUL FOR...

1. _____
2. _____
3. _____

SOMETHING I LEARNED TODAY

_____

(DRAW OR WRITE) HOW DO I FEEL TODAY?

(DRAW OR WRITE)
WHAT WAS THE BEST PART OF MY DAY?

TODAY IS _____ / _____ / _____

I'M THANKFUL FOR...

1.

2.

3.

SOMETHING I LEARNED TODAY

(DRAW OR WRITE)
HOW DO I FEEL TODAY?

WHAT WAS
THE BEST
PART OF MY
DAY?

THIS
PERSON
BROUGHT ME
JOY TODAY

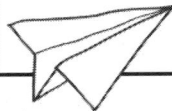

TODAY IS _____

I'M THANKFUL FOR...

1. _____
2. _____
3. _____

SOMETHING I LEARNED TODAY

_____

(DRAW OR WRITE) HOW DO I FEEL TODAY?

(DRAW OR WRITE)
WHAT WAS THE BEST PART OF MY DAY?

TODAY IS _____ / ___ / _____

I'M THANKFUL FOR...

1. _____
2. _____
3. _____

SOMETHING I LEARNED TODAY

_____

(DRAW OR WRITE) HOW DO I FEEL TODAY?

(DRAW OR WRITE)
WHAT WAS THE BEST PART OF MY DAY?

TODAY IS _____ / / _____

I'M THANKFUL FOR...

1. _____
2. _____
3. _____

SOMETHING I LEARNED TODAY

_____

(DRAW OR WRITE) HOW DO I FEEL TODAY?

(DRAW OR WRITE)
WHAT WAS THE BEST PART OF MY DAY?

TODAY IS ___ / / ___

I'M THANKFUL FOR...

1. _____

2. _____

3. _____

SOMETHING I LEARNED TODAY

_____

(DRAW OR WRITE) HOW DO I FEEL TODAY?

(DRAW OR WRITE)
WHAT WAS THE BEST PART OF MY DAY?

TODAY IS ___ / ___ / ___

I'M THANKFUL FOR...

1.

2.

3.

SOMETHING I LEARNED TODAY

(DRAW OR WRITE)
HOW DO I FEEL TODAY?

WHAT WAS THE BEST PART OF MY DAY?

THIS PERSON BROUGHT ME JOY TODAY

TODAY IS _____

I'M THANKFUL FOR...

1. _____

2. _____

3. _____

SOMETHING I LEARNED TODAY

_____

(DRAW OR WRITE) HOW DO I FEEL TODAY?

(DRAW OR WRITE)
WHAT WAS THE BEST PART OF MY DAY?

TODAY IS _____ / /

I'M THANKFUL FOR...

1. _____
2. _____
3. _____

SOMETHING I LEARNED TODAY

_____

(DRAW OR WRITE) HOW DO I FEEL TODAY?

(DRAW OR WRITE)
WHAT WAS THE BEST PART OF MY DAY?

TODAY IS _____ / / ____

I'M THANKFUL FOR...

1. _____
2. _____
3. _____

SOMETHING I LEARNED TODAY

_____

(DRAW OR WRITE) HOW DO I FEEL TODAY?

(DRAW OR WRITE)
WHAT WAS THE BEST PART OF MY DAY?

TODAY IS _____ / ___ / ___

I'M THANKFUL FOR...

1. _____

2. _____

3. _____

💡 SOMETHING I LEARNED TODAY

_____

(DRAW OR WRITE) HOW DO I FEEL TODAY?

(DRAW OR WRITE)
WHAT WAS THE BEST PART OF MY DAY?

TODAY IS ___ / ___ / ___

I'M THANKFUL FOR...

1.

2.

3.

SOMETHING I LEARNED TODAY

(DRAW OR WRITE)
HOW DO I FEEL TODAY?

WHAT WAS
THE BEST
PART OF MY
DAY?

THIS
PERSON
BROUGHT ME
JOY TODAY

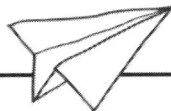

GREAT THINGS
NEVER
CAME from
COMFORT
ZONES

TODAY IS _____

I'M THANKFUL FOR...

1. _____
2. _____
3. _____

SOMETHING I LEARNED TODAY

_____

(DRAW OR WRITE) HOW DO I FEEL TODAY?

(DRAW OR WRITE)
WHAT WAS THE BEST PART OF MY DAY?

TODAY IS _____ / /

I'M THANKFUL FOR...

1. _____

2. _____

3. _____

SOMETHING I LEARNED TODAY

_____

(DRAW OR WRITE) HOW DO I FEEL TODAY?

(DRAW OR WRITE)
WHAT WAS THE BEST PART OF MY DAY?

TODAY IS ___ / ___ / ___

I'M THANKFUL FOR...

1. _____
2. _____
3. _____

SOMETHING I LEARNED TODAY

_____

(DRAW OR WRITE) HOW DO I FEEL TODAY?

(DRAW OR WRITE)
WHAT WAS THE BEST PART OF MY DAY?

TODAY IS ___/___/___

I'M THANKFUL FOR...

1.

2.

3.

SOMETHING I LEARNED TODAY

(DRAW OR WRITE)
HOW DO I FEEL TODAY?

WHAT WAS
THE BEST
PART OF MY
DAY?

THIS
PERSON
BROUGHT ME
JOY TODAY

TODAY IS _____ / /

I'M THANKFUL FOR...

1. _____
2. _____
3. _____

SOMETHING I LEARNED TODAY

_____

(DRAW OR WRITE) HOW DO I FEEL TODAY?

(DRAW OR WRITE)
WHAT WAS THE BEST PART OF MY DAY?

believe
in yourself

TODAY IS _____ / ___ / ___

I'M THANKFUL FOR...

1. _____
2. _____
3. _____

SOMETHING I LEARNED TODAY

_____

(DRAW OR WRITE) HOW DO I FEEL TODAY?

(DRAW OR WRITE)
WHAT WAS THE BEST PART OF MY DAY?

IF YOU LOVE THIS GRATITUDE JOURNAL
YOU WILL LOVE THESE OTHER CREATIVE
JOURNALS BY SELAH WORKS

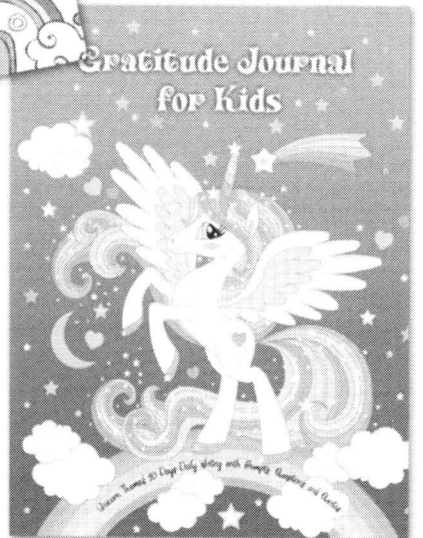

UNICORN
Activity Book
For Kids Ages 4-8

Fun Kid Workbook
Game For Learning, Coloring
Dot To Dot, Mazes, Word Search
and More!

daily
GRATITUDE JOURNAL
FOR KIDS

Children's Unicorn Themed Daily Writing with Prompts, Questions and Quotes

Sketchbook Journal For Girls

Sketchbook
for
Girls

Gratitude Journal
for Kids

Gratitude Journal 90 Days Daily Writing with Prompts, Questions and Quotes

Printed in Great Britain
by Amazon